# This Road Since Freedom

"... out of the gloomy past ...."

from Black National Anthem

Donated to
SAINT PAUL PUBLIC LIBRARY

W9-AJR-683

Books by C. Eric Lincoln

Race, Religion and the Continuing American Dilemma
The Black Church Since Frazier
The Black Experience in Religion (ed.)
The Black Muslims in America
Is Anybody Listening? (ed.)
A Pictorial History of Blackamericans (with Langston
      Hughes and Milton Meltzer)
A Profile of Martin Luther King, Jr. (ed.)
Sounds of the Struggle
The Avenue, Clayton City
The Black Church in the African American
      Experience (with Lawrence H. Mamiya)

Series Editor

The C. Eric Lincoln Series in Black Religion
      (Doubleday/Anchor Books)

A Black Theology of Liberation (James H. Cone)
Black Preaching (Henry Mitchell)
Black Religion and Black Radicalism
      (Gayraud Wilmore)
Black Sects and Cults (Joseph Washington, Jr.)
Dark Salvation (Harry V. Richardson)
Is God a White Racist? (William R. Jones)
Soul Force (Leonard E. Barrett)

# THIS ROAD SINCE FREEDOM

## Collected Poems by
## C. Eric Lincoln

Introduction by
Margaret Walker Alexander

Epilogue by
John Hope Franklin

Carolina Wren Press / Durham, North Carolina

Some of these poems have appeared in the following places:
A Room Left Over, A LIVING CULTURE IN DURHAM,
    Carolina Wren Press, 1987
A Prayer for Love, SONGS OF ZION, Parthenon Press,
    1981
How Like a Gentle Spirit, Copyright © 1989 by The United
    Methodist Publishing House. Reprinted from
    THE UNITED METHODIST HYMNAL by
    permission.


Library of Congress Cataloging-in-Publication Data
Lincoln, C. Eric (Charles Eric), 1924–
This road since freedom : collected poems / by C. Eric
Lincoln ; introduction by Margaret Walker Alexander ;
epilogue by John Hope Franklin.
p.   cm.
ISBN 0-932112-30-7—ISBN 0-932112-31-5 (pbk.)
1. Afro-Americans—Poetry.   2. Race relations—Poetry.
3. Civil rights—Poetry.   I. Title
PS3562.I472T5   1990
811'.54—dc20                                    90-33569
                                                  CIP

Copyright 1990 by C. Eric Lincoln
CAROLINA WREN PRESS is publishing this book by lease
arrangement with C. Eric Lincoln.
All rights reserved.

This book is published with funds provided in part by the
Durham Arts Council and the North Carolina Arts Council.

Cover photo by Roger Manley
Author photo by Les Todd, Duke University
Book and cover design by Martha Scotford Lange

*To those
many thousands gone
whose firm determination
to walk this road since freedom
with dignity and self-respect
helped dull some of the edges
on some of the stones
we have encountered,
and to those
whose steady commitment
to a more perfect freedom
we have yet to experience
sustains for us the vision
of a true and faithful turning
in the road ahead,
these lines are dedicated.*

C. Eric Lincoln

# Contents

# Foreword

The greatest satisfaction in life is living it; the next is thinking about it. The two go together, for reflection is the intellectual struggle to complete experience and make it whole.

This handful of lines is a part of my personal struggle to unify some fragments of experience gathered at random over more than a half century of eventful living in America. They make no claim to accumulated wisdom. Each poem reflects the struggle to interpret life, or to somehow come to terms with it at a particular moment, whether in rural Alabama of the 1940's, or some more sophisticated metropolis in the aftershock of World War II.

These poems were not written for publication, but as a personal way of responding to whatever compelled my attention and set the reflective process in motion. They are personal, for I am part of the drama I write about. But they also make an effort to interpret reality through other eyes I know about.

Honoring me by lending their names to this small volume are long-time friends, Margaret Walker Alexander and John Hope Franklin. Dr. Alexander, who wrote *Jubilee*, and who is equally well-known for her poetry, has been gracious enough to write the introduction to this work. Dr. Franklin, whose celebrated history, *From Slavery to Freedom*, has informed two generations about a critical period in African-American development, has generously written an epilogue. I am grateful to them for their confidence; and I absolve them of any blame for whatever failings or disappointments this effort may entail.

Finally, I acknowledge with appreciation a very considerable debt to Dolores Jones-Morehead, who faithfully and capably prepared this manuscript for publication; and to my family, for they continue to be my most difficult critics, my most ardent supporters, and my most compelling motivation.

> C. Eric Lincoln
> Kumasi Hill
> Hillsborough, North Carolina

# Introduction

I welcome the opportunity to write a few words of introduction for this quite interesting collection of poetry. C. Eric Lincoln is a scholar of great repute. His monumental work on *The Black Muslims in America* followed by his work on the Black Church earned him a solid place in American Letters. It is therefore quite refreshing to see another side, a poetic side, of this prolific scholar and author.

These are poems written over a period of forty years during which the intellectual ferment and social upheaval in the United States left deep impressions on the psyches of Americans. They are almost privately personal, yet social in a very national way; mostly lyrical and yet occasionally narrative and dramatic. What impresses me most is that they record a vulnerability as well as sensitivity to what is positive and beautiful as well as what is poignantly painful in American society.

The poet's racial experience is most passionately reflected where the poems are most eloquent, as in "This Road Since Freedom," but there are religious lyrics too, the "Eighth Psalm" and "The Church of God," for example. Some poems are briefly personal love and nature lyrics. In fact love is a thematic thread running throughout the volume. Some, like the declaratory "125th Street Rap Session," are boldly dramatic and interpretative.

The poet speaks in his own voice with a deft technique and a clear perspective on the American scene. My first reaction was to see this work as a medley of ideas maturing over many years, occasions, comments and impressions. Where is the unifying element or the pole of meaning around which they are integrated, I asked myself. And then I realized the title is itself the fundamental focus of the work: *This Road Since Freedom.*

The Black Experience offers a many-faceted perspective on American life. No two people see the same events and circumstances in the same way. What is valuable always is to know another individual's prism and to be able to see reality through his eyes. I think you will find that challenge rewarding as you encounter it in this volume.

Margaret Walker Alexander
Jackson, Mississippi

*My poems derive from the life I know . . . .*

**Langston Hughes**

# PART I

## THE PILGRIMAGE

# THE DERELICT

I am alone,
alone I must make my way.
Struggle alone
out of the night to day.

I am the son of America
　　　but America has denied me.
I am a free citizen
　　　but I am denied civil privileges.
I am a man
　　　but my face is black. . . .

　　　　　　What of that?
　　　　　　Did not God create
　　　　　　black faces and white,
　　　　　　yellow faces and brown
　　　　　　to be brothers
　　　　　　all . . . ?

I will seek my God
and he will grant me audience;
He will see the injustices I suffer.
God has not intended that I should be
scorned,
lynched,
kicked
and broken in the dust.
It is not God's will that I should be
humiliated before my children,
who understanding nothing,
cry aloud in anguish
and fill the night with tears.
It is not God's will
that my life should forever be a pawn
in the hands of men without honor
and without faith
in the truth of his Word,
the righteousness of his Law.

For in the beginning
did not God
cast all men in a single mould?

No man above another
but man to man a brother.

I cried out to God;
on bended knees I sought my maker
in the quiet peace of the chapel,
in the majesty of the fields, the woodlands,
in the tortured roar of the city streets,
I breathed a prayer.
And in the silent night
when doors are shut and men are equal
I sought the Lord
Almighty God.

To God I took my case
and left it folded on the altar.

God did not answer,
God hid his face.

My God, my God,
why hast Thou forsaken me?

They told me there was a God,
a God of Mercy,
a God of Justice,
a God of Compassion,
a God of Love
who answers the prayers
of men in anguish and distress,
who knows no fear,
who shows no favor,
but in whose hand
are the balances
on which men's souls are judged.

Ah, tell me
did they lie?
Is there no Mercy?
Is there no Justice?
Is there no Compassion?
Where is God?

I am alone,
alone I must make my way.
Struggle alone
out of the night to day.

*1953*

# AT MIDNIGHT

## (When the Children Cry)

At midnight
when the children cry,
the anguished sound of sobbing,
half-muted
in the dank and rancid pillows,
embarrasses the night,
and tears
flow unrestrained
from swollen eyes
and lacerated souls.

Too innocent to understand
or curse the wantonness of men,
the children lie bewildered
in the dark
and weeping splotch idealistic white
with grey.

Clasping finally their
unclenched hands
they pray:

> Dear God,
> to be as other children . . . now
> the Cross, the Flag are mine somehow.

The night is cold
or warm, no matter;
the stellar light of heaven
indicts the guilty earth
and shines no more.

And in the dark
there is no answer
why it is that prejudice
and
hate

should mock God's
Second Admonition.

The young and tender eyes
that see by day
how man receives his brother
by night are filled with tears.

O that the Law of all the Cosmos
governing the circling stars,
the orbits of the mighty suns
that shine beyond
this hate-wracked world we know,
could somehow bridle man,
if bridled man must be.
O that the lacerations that are ours
shall somehow die with us
and pass not to our children,
the tender souls that haunt the night
with weeping,
that shame the night with tears.

*1954*

# SPIRIT OF '76

White men, Black men fought and died
that all men might be free.
But when the fighting was all done,
and when the victory was won,
Who gained the jubilee,
Who gained the jubilee?

The whites who lived,
the blacks who died
were set at liberty.

*1975*

# THE PILGRIMAGE

Africa, Mother Africa,
I come at last to thee.
O ancient land of mystic fame,
O land from whence my fathers came
across the Western Sea—
what do you hold for me?
what is my legacy?

Africa, Mother Africa,
Your God my fathers knew,
before the Western strangers came,
before I lost my father's name,
my spirit dwelt with you.
O land my fathers knew,
my spirit longs for you.

Africa, Mother Africa,
I stand upon your shore.
I hear the drums' pervasive plea,
I hear my fathers calling me
above the breakers' roar—
Come home for evermore,
Come home for evermore.

Africa, Mother Africa,
The centuries have flown.
But ever have I yearned to see
the Motherland that gave to me,
out of the vast unknown,
the heritage I own.

Africa
O Africa
My Africa.

*1969*

# RECONCILIATION

Give me your hand, my Brother,
give me your hand.
Divided we fall, my Brother,
together we stand.
Come, let's forget the past:
a lie that could not hope to last.
It's gone my Brother;
let us cast
our lot as one.

Give me your hand; it's white
and mine is black.
Together let's hold high the light
that must guide back
America: far out to sea,
lost in the fog that slavery
cast over you and me.
We'll find the sun.

*1954*

# PART II

## OFF MAIN

# POLITICAL RALLY

The bugles and the drums
are hushed;
the guitars twang
a last refrain.
The guests of honor
have arrived.
The good ol' boys
are rounding up
the motley crowd
turned out
for the occasion.

Come closer, friends,
come closer.
Closer,
if you please!

The hollow ring
that chills the solemn air
is the echo
of the politicians' craft.
Their word facades
are gaudy:
like jungle birds
they strut
and squawk
and clamor.

Promise heaven-with-a-bridge
arching majestically
across the azure sky,
far above the numb and colorless
gray reality
of hemlock-bitter life on earth
where hunger is
and prejudice
and hate
and empty souls,

wide-mouthed
with throats dust-caked,
stand gawking
in the shadows
and the gloom.

Despairing of God and meaning
still they wait
as if to ride some eternal carousel.
They wait until
the frenzied vapors of the politicians
fill them up
with rainbow-crystal promises
that burst and vanish
one against the other
ere they touch
the dull and broken edges
of mangled hopes
long since expired.

They wait
in wistful gasconade:
eyes hard against
the wonderous golden span
that oratory built
across the raw abyss
that separates the status quo
from Shangri-La.

Confused and titillated by it all
soon they will shout "Hurrah"
and pledge their emptiness.

So is their dreariness compounded,
even as they cheer
in momentary frenzy,
flinging their hats a moment
ere they fall silent
and go creeping back
to empty lives they have not left.

*1946*

# 125TH STREET RAP SESSION

Listen to me Brothers, I'm gonna tell it like it is,
Why you don't get your percentage while The Man is gettin' his.
Now it ain't no great big secret, and it ain't no mystery,
You peed on the pumpkin, Brothers, when you forgot your history.

> Well, rap on, Brother!
> I got to lay it on the wood.
> Rap right on, Brother!
> Listen to me. Listen good.

>> 'Cause you don't have to scratch
>> An' you don't have to grin.
>> Scratchin' without itchin'
>> Is a vee-nial sin!

Now you read in the Bible about the First Creation.
Well it don't even mention this here civilization
But they dug up the world to find the Very First Man,
An' Brothers, lo and behold, **he was a black African!**

> Well, rap on, Brother!
> He was in Tanganyiki.
> Rap right on, Brother!
> He had on a Dashiki!

>> Now they were so disappointed
>> When they saw he was black,
>> They dug another big hole
>> And tried to put him right back!

Back in fourteen hundred, and around ninety-two
Ol' Columbus was looking for something jazzy to do.
He told Queen Izzy, "I'll be diggin' you later,
I got to try the Big Atlantic with my black navigator."

> Well, rap on, Brother!
> His name was Pedro 'Lonzo Nino.
> Rap right on, Brother!
> He was a solid black bambino!

Now Lonnie looked at his compass,
And gave his tiller a whirl,
And the first thing you know,
They had a brand new world!

The big Injun chiefs came out to meet 'em in style
So Columbus and Lonnie stuck around for awhile.
When they split back to Spain—ol' Lonnie still at the helm,
Well Old Queen Isabella made them Knights of the Realm!

Well, rap on, Brother!
They had a shipload of gold.
Rap right on, Brother!
It was a sight to behold!

They sent the Spanish Army
All the way to Peru
An' in every expedition
They had some Brothers just like you!

De Olana with Balboa, Narvaez had Estevan.
Black heroes fought every battle from Peru to Rio Grande.
Planted wheat in Colorado—first this country'd ever seen.
Helped destroy the Aztec Empire; helped to build St. Augustine!

Well, rap on, Brother!
If someone had kept the score . . .
Rap right on, Brother!
Yours would be "Conquistador"!

Before the Mayflower
Ever left England's shore,
We'd been ramblin' 'round this country
For a century or more.

But the Anglos heard the music so they got into the act,
Came and killed off all the Injuns before they got hip to the fact
That this cotton and tobacco did not intend to raise itself,
So they put the Blacks in bondage and the Injuns on the shelf.

Well, rap on, Brother!
Well, that's the way it began.
Rap right on, Brother!
Said you were three-fifths of a man!

> But Nat Turner was a preacher,
> Hated slavery worse than sin.
> Called his sword his Freedom Bible,
> Killed a hundred slavery men!

Now Doctor DuBois went to Harvard, you know.
He was hip to the ivy, so he purloined the show.
He dressed like a diplomat, he sported a cane,
Had a Van Dyke beard and an Einstein brain!

> Well, rap on, Brother!
> Ol' DuBois had big thunder.
> Rap right on, Brother!
> He put the world on a wonder!

> He dug the Big Books
> And wrote a few of his own.
> Couldn't nobody touch him
> 'Cause that cat was real gone!

But don't forget about ol' Booker Tee,
Elijah Muhammad and Marcus Gar-vee,
Martin the Magnificent, Malcolm the Prince,
Thurgood Marshall for the Brothers' defense.

> Well, rap on, Brother!
> Say you're black and you're proud!
> Rap right on, Brother!
> Let's hear you say it out loud!

> Now black is your heritage,
> And it's got to be right!
> 'Cause your history ain't something
> That got started last night.

If you know where you come from, you oughta know where
  you're goin'.
If you know how you got here, you know you got to keep rowin'.
It ain't no big secret—it's the same first and last,
You ain't got no future if you don't know your past.

  Well, rap on, Brother!
  Well that's the way the bunny hops.
  Rap right on, Brother!
  An' that's the way the pickle pops.

    You don't have to scratch
    And you don't have to smile.
    Baby, grinnin' and scratchin'
    Have gone out of style!

    Yeah! Grinnin' and scratchin'
    Is clean out of style!

Now, Brothers and Sisters,
Y'all dig me where I'm coming from?

*1967*

# A ROOM LEFT OVER

Mama
Mama
Why can't we move
Why can't we move
And have a house
With two real beds
Or maybe even three
So you could
Have one
And not have to sleep with anybody
When you don't feel so good
Sometimes
Because you're old
And kinda tired
Mama?

Mama
Mama
I don't want to sleep with Sonny
And Jim
And Eva
Anymore
Because
My teacher said
That boys and girls
Ought not to sleep together
In just one bed
And Eva is a girl
Mama.

Mama
Mama
Why can't we move
Why can't we move
And have a great big house
That's got four rooms
And have a bed

For Sonny and Jim and me
In one room
And another bed
For you and Eva
In another room
And we could cook and eat
In another room
Mama
And have
A room left over.

Mama
Mama
And maybe we could
Put some pictures on the wall
And have a toilet
And not have to go
To the john down the hall
When Mr. Luke's been drinking
Or Louise from upstairs
Is in there with the cramps
Or old Miss Seely
Is stuck down in the tub
'Cause she's so old
And fat.

But Mama
Mama
If you don't really want to
We don't have to move
When you don't feel so good
You can sleep
In my place
And maybe
You won't be so tired
And hurt so much.

And
Mama
You don't have to worry
Ain't nobody
Going to tell that nosy teacher
Nothing about
What ain't her business
Nohow!

But
Mama
Mama
Why can't we move?

*1957*

# OFF MAIN

I walked off Main a block or so today.
I saw a sight that turned my heart away:
a youth of twenty in the gutter lay.

Dressed a la mode, from feathered hat to shoes,
bespattered coat of many gaudy hues.
A fashion-piece for passers-by reviews.

He lay there moaning, features pale as death;
God's heir to wisdom, holiness and health
lay senseless there with alcoholic breath.

*1942*

# DIXIE IN HARLEM

Nigger boy settin' at a white man's desk,
posin' a white man's pose.
Nigger boy drivin' a white man's car,
wearin' a white man's clothes.
Nigger boy goin' to a white man's school—
       Watch out there Nigger, don't be no fool;
       'Sa white world, anyhow!
Dixie cracker on a Harlem Street
lookin' for some fun.
Dixie cracker wants a Nigger girl;
he is his daddy's son.
       Mister, you're far from your lynchin' crowd;
       Move on out and don't breathe too loud.
You ain't in Dixie now!

*1944*

# TO J.T.W.

Your sons are we, and rare our claim
for we profess no common name
nor claim a common race or creed,
but in our common hour of need
as youth you touched us, bade us rise
to test our wings against the skies.

Your sons are we, the orphans maimed
the world impatiently disclaimed,
yet with whose pregnable estate
you cast the lot that challenged fate.
And mentor, advocate and friend,
Taught us the lineaments of men.

The years have ripened, time has sped
and youth's insouciance has fled.
Our dreams are done, each cup is filled
with what was destined, what was willed.
The blossom from the bud has blown;
as bent the twig, the tree has grown.

Some marks we missed—by less or more,
impartial time will post the score.
But every shaft that flew was spent
with thoughtful purpose, true intent.
Your sons are we, and in your name
No mark was higher than our aim.

*1979*

# TO A BLACK ARTIST

Paint on, black artist! deft your strokes and proud,
heed not the mindless passage of the crowd.
And if your works engrace no hall of fame
nor garner honorifics to your name,
true to yourself your art must ever be,
for only truth can set the conscience free.
Paint on! Paint on! achieve your grand design
Stroke by bold stroke, and line by fateful line.

Man's inhumanity to man your urgent theme:
harsh is the life in pursuit of a dream—
a people maimed and tortured by the goad
in cheerless struggle on a cheerless road,
strange fruit that hangs from ever-silent trees,
strong prayers that rise from ever-patient knees.
Refresh your palette with their blood and stress;
limn your great mural with their faithfulness.

Paint on, black artist! hang your canvas high:
the whole world will be your gallery by-and-by.
Your theme in human councils shall be heard
for truth will not forever be deferred.
Paint on, black artist! that the world may see
A nobler race than yours is yet to be.

*1945*

# PART III

---

## LEGACY

# RETROSPECTION

Look back if you would read the course ahead
for past and future in life's grand design
are tethered by one solitary line
and what will be is anchored in what was
for nothing is except it finds its cause
in what has gone before.

The line that separates the false and true
distinguishes what is from what is not,
yet holds them interface, a single lot;
and past and present on one frame depend
for what's begun determines what will end
and reckons not the score.

Look back and then resume your forward way;
schooled by the night, anticipate the day.

*1981*

# THE DEBT

What is it that dwells within my soul,
that bids me climb the steep and crumbling stair
to dizzy heights, to seek a distant goal,
to realize a castle built on air?

What is it that urges forward still
though dark the night and treacherous is the way?
What is it that stronger than my will
bids me toil on when I would stop and play?

A restless something surging in my breast
implores me, whispers, pleads incessantly,
that I must reach the top ere I may rest
to justify those who have faith in me.

*1942*

# INDIFFERENT AGE

I shall not care when I am old
and life has crept behind the wall to die.
When youth's vain pleasures dim my aged eye
and senile organs spawn but senile mold,
I shall not care.

I shall not care when comes the day
that feverish love and sex no longer charm;
bare, numbered days shall cause me no alarm.
'Twill matter not: for I have passed this way,
I shall not care.

*1950*

# LACERATIONS

The great Minds in the universities
writing new books
cryptic.

And the egg-headed students
trying to understand the old,
the Great Conversation.

You
Doctors of Philosophy
Doctors of Psychology
Doctors of Theology
Can you point us to a little love,
a little appreciation
of what we are
or even what we hope to be?

*1952*

# SO HIGH, SO DEEP, SO WIDE

I do not seek a life
in which there are no peaks or valleys.
Let there be order, but
spare me the tedium of sameness,
the boredom of predictability.

Let there be contrasts in my life.

Let there be heights:
majestic as the mountains,
by-roads to the stars.
Let there be depths:
mysterious as the oceans,
engaging as the whirlpool,
exciting as the storm.
Let there be breadth:
endless as the prairies,
tethering the far horizon,
stretched between the mountains
and the sea.

Let life be
so high
so deep
so wide
that though every dimension
exceeds my possibilities,
nothing obscures the challenge
to show myself undaunted,
to live life in perspective
with gratitude
and grace.

*1978*

# WHO'S WHO

When Death visits
he does not choose a man
because he is poor.
The call to judgment
is not contingent upon
the arch of your nose,
the shape of your head,
the curl of your hair.
It does not matter
if you are a Baptist
or Catholic,
Democrat,
or Republican,
White,
Black—
no matter.
You may be a professor,
ditch-digger,
an atheistic deep sea diver,
a hillbilly,
or a debutante.

Sooner or later
Death comes.

When we expire
we all return to dust
they say.
One dust:
the particles of which are forever blown about
by the Four Winds of the earth.
Forever mingled—
the rich with the poor,
the high and the lowly.

And color is not a factor,
name is not an issue.

So, after all,
in the final analysis,
does it really matter so much
Who's Who?

*1944*

# LEGACY

When I have lived my life and come to die,
bedeck me not in finery for the gaze
of curious crowds with sympathetic eye
who knew me not—nor marked my earthly ways.
Nor would I have you shed a single tear—
for life's a ransomless commodity.
We all must one day end the sojourn here
and someday render up to Death his fee.

When I shall come to die, the flowers you bring
were better left to cheer those who remain.
And all the mournful hymns the choir may sing
will never bring my soul to earth again.
But if on earth I sought the good, the true,
I shall not fear the time my soul must fly.
And my unfinished quest I leave to you,
and falter not when it is time to die.

*1949*

# RELEASE

Come to me gently, O Death . . .
Cool, with the comfort of evening;
wipe from the rim of my brow
the sweat of oppression and sorrow.
Fold on the wreck of my breast
that once heaved with suppressed emotion
gnarled, ugly hands that have known
toil in the muck of life's trenches:
hands that have toiled without pay
under the false lash of color.
Fold them together, O Death,
upon my breast in peace.

*1950*

# ON BEING MYSELF

I want to be the self I want to be,
the self that lets my inner light shine through for me,
the self that lets me be the self I am,
that leaves me free to swim above the dam.
I want to be the self that sets me free
that lets me find the existential me.

I want to be the self that says to me,
"Your moment here is your eternity.
Go kiss a rose; go travel to a star;
go build a bridge that spans the near and far."
I want to be the self I'm meant to be:
the self for which my life was lent to me.

*1978*

# PART IV

## DEFT ENCOUNTER

# ATLANTA GIRL

When night unfolds her tender veil of blue,
My arms will hold you, Atlanta Girl.
Beneath the stars we'll pledge our love anew,
The moon will lend us its spell.

When shadows fall across the closing day,
My lips will find you, Atlanta Girl.
When with the dawn the shadows steal away,
A kiss must seal our farewell.

O winds that hurry by
Pause in your silent flight.
O tell my love that I
Wait here tonight.
Stars up above the world
Shining so merrily
Keep my Atlanta Girl
Safe, safe for me.

Stars up above the world
Shining so merrily
Keep my Atlanta Girl
Safe for me.

*1956*

# TWO LOVERS

I saw two lovers
in the soft enchantment
of a summer night—
two youthful lovers.

A man:
bold as a lion
roaring in the dawn,
fierce in his passion,
confident in his prowess,
tender as the breeze
that kissed their trysting place.

A woman:
radiant in her ecstasy,
demanding in her surrender,
timing her rhythm to
the silent drums
pulsing down the centuries of creation.

Ah, young lovers,
Beautiful is your love,
Beautiful are you.

*1944*

# LITTLE LUCY

Every Friday afternoon
I saw you
hopscotching in the churchyard
across from my apartment:
your cheering squad of urchins
from the ghetto around Dudley Station
proclaiming your expertise
in a cacophony of screams.

I was not impressed.

Every Saturday afternoon
I heard you
debating the church organ
with your Sunshine Gospel Chorus:
that motley crew of demons
in sacrificial halos,
sing-songing plaintively,
their reedy little voices
augmented by your own.

A bit off-key
it seemed to me.

Every Friday,
Every Saturday
my work came to a halt,
my concentration shattered
by all that noise you mothered
over in the churchyard
across the narrow street
from where I sat
hovering over a portable
long since silent,
half-forgotten
in my reverie.

Even when
I closed the window
and drew the blinds
I could not shut you out.

The old landlady
worn down and crippled
hobbled by my open door
and worried that
my industry had ceased.
And when she learned
the reason why
she smiled,
dismissing my exasperation:
A crooked finger
pressed against her lips
compelled my silence.

Oh, Sir! she said
(a fluorescent pleasure
twinkling her tired old eyes)—
Oh, Sir, Professor Sir,
you must mean
our Little Lucy!
That's our little lady
comes every Friday evening
and every Saturday morning
to help out with the children.
Oh, Sir, Professor Sir,
don't you know
Our Little Lucy?

She's just the sweetest thing!

A college degree, she's got, Sir,
and another
from the Conservatory, too.
And she teaches second grade
off in Springfield, I think it is.
She is just the nicest thing!

Comes home, she does,
on the weekend
to be with her Aunty,
(that's Big Lucy, you know, Sir)
and she helps with the children
at the church, she does.

She is the sweetest little thing!

I wished aloud
(and somewhat irreverently, perhaps)
that their Little Lucy
(She's the noisiest little thing!)
would spend two or three weekends
in Springfield.

I had a book to write.

But Old Lady Bailey
brought Little Lucy over
to be met.
See for yourself,
she said,
Ain't she the sweetest thing?

She was.

And what is more,
before the summer
could change its mood,
we were married.

Time has flown.

Now every afternoon
Monday to Sunday, it is,
I have in my house
a motley pair of urchins
who look like me,

somewhat,
and more like
Little Lucy.

Thank you,
Little Lucy. Thank you.
Though I may never write a book
I am content with just one line:

You are the sweetest thing—
Ever!

*1973*

# CONTINGENCY

If you were my love
the why would stand revealed
and I could read with some discernment
the sacred mysteries . . .
the blurred and shifting characters written in the clay
that is my life—some purpose there to find,
some consecrated way.
For surely God (and God must be) is wise
and He has not in reckless promiscuity
created for a mere beguile the earth and skies . . .
and you and me.
And if you were my love
would not his purpose then reveal itself
to us—the prisoners in the cave . . . ?
And what other could my role in this creation be
except to be your slave?

If you were my love
there would no cloud the blue horizon mar.
And all the limitless expanse the heavens know,
a world each star,
the celestial eminence,
would never know the frightening roll of thunder
nor send down
the lightning flash that stills the soul;
Nor rain, nor cold, nor storm . . .
but only warmth: the kiss of moonlight,
the music of the wind.

And if you were my love
my breast no longer could my heart contain,
for it must leap the broadest rivers
and dance upon the hills to
winds that pluck the strings that hold
this vast infinity of worlds in grand array.

Then all the ugliness of men in search of gain,
and all the malformations,
the recondite . . .
would be manifest in beauty in this my perfect hour
as when the sun ascends at break of day,
or when the stars push back the veil of night -
If you were my love . . .
If you would be
my love.

*1957*

# DEFT ENCOUNTER

Across the wastelands
of my loneliness,
threading the steaming canyons
of the city streets,
you make your way
to where I wait
ensconced in the fastness
of my Lilliputian aerie,
high among competing towers
of stone and glass.
I revel in my solitude
and wait your signal
at the door.

You've come;
the evening sets its own agenda.
At first like mindless puppets
we posture and react
as if on cue
from some master mind
beyond our own ordaining:
our deft little games
of whether/whether not
to be/or be undone
be/not to be.

All the shibboleths
we learned so well
define the boundaries
of your deft encounter,
declaring who and what we are
or what we will to be,
perceived to be.
But every shibboleth
is eroded by its recitation
and the fearsome gargoyles
leering from the ramparts of restraint
to guard the shrines we worship in

soon sway and totter,
cringe and fall,
loosened from their ancient bondstones
by the tremulousness of love.

Love disarmed requires no armor.
Dark little confessions,
traded in love's afterglow,
in child-like confidence and trust,
mark our progress to Elysium.
The innocence of intimacy is ours.
O where were you a world or two ago?
Time was so young
and I had just begun to be.
Time was/time is,
today eclipses
all the yesterdays
that might have been
and if tomorrow comes
it will be today eternalized.

Our promises against tomorrow
etched in deft caresses
flourished with a momentary tear
that glistens boldly
for one fateful moment,
challenging the awesomeness
of time and space.
Until tomorrow comes
we shall be holding hands
across a continent,
weathering the winter,
waiting for the spring,
to verify love wrenched from the void,
a memorable encounter,
and make it live again.

Outside the city sleeps
and dawn begins her mystic revels with the sky,

but here within my rock-bound caravanserai
peace reigns supreme.
The rhythms of your being
beat steadily in tandem with my own;
your silent breath upon my cheek
confirms that this is not a dream
but life, your life and mine,
melded for a fateful moment
in one eternity.
And as the sunlight
stalks the furtive shadows in my room,
my lips perform
the prayer my heart designs
in thankfulness that you have come to me,
and touching once again
your tousled hair,
I join you in your sleep.

*1989*

# SWEET MOTHER

Sweet mother of my unborn child,
dear flower, for me pale and wan,
an Eden mine: no more a wild
and wasted life, a bright new dawn
is mine to welcome, fresh with dew
of care and kindliness of you.

My rough uncultured tongue can ne'er
describe the ecstasy my soul
has known and reveled in when e'er
I've raised to fervid lips the bowl
of living, sweetened with the mild
and hopeful waiting for your child.

*1962*

# JOYCE

Mothered in the bosom of the night
a million stars look down with sleepy eyes
from heaven's vaulted temple of the skies,
when in her sleep
she smiles.

*1953*

# PART V

# RETURN, O LORD

# A PRAYER FOR LOVE

Lord, let me love; let loving be the symbol
Of grace that warms my heart; and let me find
Thy loving hand to still me when I tremble
At Thy command to love all humankind.
Lord, let me love—though love may be the losing
Of every earthly treasure I possess.
Lord, make Thy love the pattern of my choosing
And let Thy will dictate my happiness.

I have no wish to wield the sword of power,
I want no man to leap at my command,
Nor let my critics feel constrained to cower
For fear of some reprisal at my hand.
Lord, teach me mercy; let me be the winner
Of every man's respect and simple love
For I have known Thy mercy, though a sinner,
Whenever I have sought Thy peace above.

Lord, let me love the lowly and the humble,
Forgetting not the mighty and the strong.
And give me grace to love those who may stumble,
Nor let me seek to judge of right or wrong.
Lord, let my parish be the world unbounded
By any vain pretense of race or clan.
Let every hateful doctrine be confounded
That interdicts the love of man for man.

*1958*

# THE EIGHTH PSALM

O Lord, how perfect is Thy name,
In all the earth how great Thy fame!
Above the heavens Thou didst set
Thy glory, gracious Lord, and yet
Out of the mouths of babes calls Thee
Thy strength to still the enemy!

When I behold Thy heavens so grand,
The moon and stars at Thy command,
Lord, what is man that Thou shouldst heed
His call, or visit with his seed?
Near angels Thou has fixed his stead,
Honor and glory crown his head.

O'er all Thy works man rules complete.
All things Thou placed beneath his feet:
Birds of the air, beasts of the field,
The fish that swim the seas must yield.
O Lord, our Lord, how great Thy name!
Throughout the earth, how wide Thy fame!

Amen.

*1958*

# RETURN, O LORD

Dear Lord, I am bewildered by the angry world.
I do not know the meaning of the flags unfurled.
The noisy skies, the tortured seas:
What sayest Thou, O Lord, to these?

I hear the strident call to arms; above the scenes
Of men in desperate debate, their war machines
Defile the skies, pollute the earth.
How much, O Lord, can peace be worth?

Hast Thou in merited disgust turned back from man
Who recklessly has broken trust and sinned again?
Forgive our selfish lust for power
And save us in this dreadful hour.

Return, O Lord, return and save this wretched race,
Save us, not by Thy justice Lord, but by Thy grace,
Forgive our foolish, pompous way,
And save us from ourselves, we pray.

*1944*

# THE CHURCH OF GOD

The Church of God must now prevail
Against the world's divisive scheme.
The mighty strength of union pales
The Adversary of the Dream.

The Church of God must now prevail:
No breach deform its sacred walls.
When storms of hate and doubt assail,
Let love and peace reign in its halls.

The love of God must now prevail:
Christ spoke the love of God for man.
And loving God, love cannot fail
To transcend every racial wall.

The peace of God must now prevail:
In Christ shall wars and hatreds end.
The arms of earth cannot avail
The peace of heav'n alone can win.

The reign of God must now prevail:
Let selfish strivings be undone.
Across the world His name we hail—
Our Lord and King, the Risen Son!

*1953*

60

# HOW LIKE A GENTLE SPIRIT

How like a gentle spirit deep within
God reigns our fervent passions day by day
And gives us strength to challenge and to win
Despite the perils of our chosen way.

Let God be God wherever life may be
Let every tongue bear witness to his call
All humankind is one by God's decree
Let God be God. Let God be God for us all.

God, like a mother eagle, hovers near
On mighty wings of power manifest
God like a gentle shepherd stills our fear
And comforts us against a peaceful breast.

When in our vain pretensions we conspire
To shape God's image as we see our own
Hark to the voice above our base desire
God is the sculptor, we the broken stone.

Through all our fretful claims of sex and race
The universal love of God shines through
For God is love transcending style and place
And all the idle options we pursue.

*1987*

*Copyright © 1989 by The United Methodist Publishing House.*
*Reprinted from THE UNITED METHODIST HYMNAL by permission.*

# HAIL BETHEL

### I

Hail to thee, O Mother Bethel, In thy name we gather here
Ancient refuge of our fathers from the storms of doubt and fear
Thou the sign of our redemption, rescue from travail untold
Symbol of God's might ransom, dearer far to us than gold.

### Chorus

So we march forth, O Bethel, in thy name
Yes we march in the shadow of the pillar of fire
For the Lord God who marches at our head is the same
Who didst strike our chains of bondage and ransom us entire.

We shall march, Mother Bethel, by thy grace
We shall sound forth the trumpets triumphant everyday
For the Lord God who favors us and shows us his face
Has made this church a nation and sent us on our way.

### II

When the curse of bondage smothered Christian witness in the land
And our piteous cries for mercy met rebuff on every hand
God's apostle did revive us, preaching faith and freedom true
Raised a church that shook a nation, taught the world what grace
    can do.

### III

Courage Bethel, God has called you, far from Afric's mystic land,
To a mission he ordainest, to fulfill his sacred plan
Through a glass we see but darkly, trusting Him that by His grace
When in faith our work concluded, we shall see Him face to face.

## IV

High your honor, Mother Bethel, we rejoice to speak your name
Though the centuries rise and vanish, age to age thou art the same
Gathering thy faithful children, binding up the wounds of time
Praising God for His compassion, making life in Christ sublime.

## V

Lift your mighty voice, O Bethel, let your jubilation rise
Let the joy of your salvation echo through the vaulted skies
Praise the lord of grace and glory, Hallelujah! to the throne
In his bosom God has kept you safe and blameless for His own.

## VI

Lo, thy steady hand has kept us in the straight and narrow way
Serving friend and foe together, grateful for each precious day
When the morning breaks asunder and the days and nights
    shall cease
When the judgment has been rendered we shall know eternal peace.

### (Alternate Chorus)

Ever onward! Ever upward! Lead us forth in grand array
Faithful to your high commission, falter not along the way
Bethel, God be ever with you as he was in days of yore
Forward into God's great future He will bless you evermore.

*1987*

*Commissioned for the 200th anniversary of the AME Church; Performed at
Kennedy Center, 1987*

# MOTHER'S DAY

Dear Mother, on this Mother's Day
Whose life has not been touched with fame
The world may scarcely know your name
Your hair is kissed with silver gray
But you're a mother just the same.

Brave Mother, on this Mother's Day
You bear the secrets of the years
You've lived with hopes and cares and fears
And washed each soul that went astray
As mothers do, with mothers' tears.

Sweet Mother, on this Mother's Day
You take no thought of all the pain
That you have borne; who can't explain
Your sacrifices, nor can say
When you will sacrifice again.

O God, in Thine own sacred way
Bless her with thy divine embrace
Whose virtue wreathes her seasoned face
Let every day be Mother's Day
With miracles of boundless grace.

*1960*

# PEACE IS OUR MISSION,
# LOVE IS OUR TRUTH

Hark how the tumult burdens the breeze
'Round us the darkness falls cold and damp
The mountains shudder, fire roils the seas
God bear us safely to Zion's camp.

Though there be wars and rumors of wars
Scourging the earth and wasting our youth
Faith must not falter, eyes on the stars
Peace is our mission, love is our truth.

For true compassion long cast aside
For vile transgressions, for spiteful tongue
For justice broken, for love denied
God's righteous judgment ponders our wrong.

Nations and empires rise and decline
Princes and prelates rule for a day
God reigns forever, His grand design
Girded by grace shall not pass away.

Stand forth ye faithful, dare to be true
Lay down your arms, your ensigns revoke
God's first commandment calls out to you
Above the clamor, the fire and the smoke.

Hold back the judgment, Great God, we pray
Though we have scorned to walk in thy path
Grant us thy mercy yet for a day
Hold back by justice, spare us thy wrath.

*1987*

# WE SHALL BE ONE AGAIN

Into each life the pause of death must come
Each in their time, God calls the blessed home
Strong in our faith it falls our lot to mourn
Those whom we love who from our midst are torn.

We shall be one again and we will share
In heaven's rapture that they savor there
Like them when once our final course is run
We'll hear the gentle Master say, "Well done!"

The Book of Life is tallied page by page
The trumpet sounds alike for every age
And soon or late, and whether near or far
We all must bow before the evening star.

Hark to the trumpet's call to rest and peace
God in His grace grants us His sweet release
Farewell to those whose time God did ordain
Our faith confirmed, we shall be one again.

We shall be one again just as before
In sweet communion on that other shore
Praise be to God that when our course is run
We'll be together evermore as one.

*1987*

# PART VI

## THE LEGEND OF NIGGER CHARLEY

# THE LEGEND OF NIGGER CHARLEY

Here's the story of a brother
Who rode the western range
But the cowboys used to treat him
Like a coyote with the mange.
They all called him Nigger Charley
Just like he didn't have a name
'Til he upped and pulled his forty-four
And evened up the game.

Now one day he ordered whiskey
In Dutch Cassidy's saloon.
The bartender he allowed
He'd rather die than serve a coon.
Charley figured to oblige him
Seeing as how he put the case;
Shucked a bullet through his gizzard
So's to save his ugly face.

Charley, cock your long black pistol,
Look that varmint in the eye;
If he got a right to cuss you,
Then he got a right to die.
Charley, cock your long black pistol,
Level down your forty-four;
Don't you never let nobody
Desecrate your name no more.

Quicker than it takes to tell it
They marched Charley off to jail,
But the Dutchman left short-handed
Went and got him out on bail.
So the marshal said to Charley,
"'Bliged if you don't stray too far,
Since you plugged the late bartender
Reck'n you aim to keep the bar."

Charley called his hand and raised him
Pouring whiskey day by day;
As the years went drifting by him
Fame and fortune came his way.
Wooed and won the Dutchman's daughter,
Cactus flower of the West,
Diamond horseshoe in his collar,
Chain of nuggets 'cross his vest.

When the cowboys came to frolic
At Dutch Cassidy's saloon
Every glass was raised to Charley;
Charley called the dance and tune.
Ain't no varmint never called him
Nigger Charley anymore
Since the day he upped the ante
With a smoking forty-four.

*1972*

# BALLAD OF PEACHTREE STREET

New York has got Fifth Avenue,
They say it's hard to beat.
L.A.'s got Wilshire Boulevard
But Atlanta's got Peachtree Street.
I've never seen Fifth Avenue,
Nor Wilshire, by the way,
But I've seen the sights on Peachtree
Where the Georgia Peaches play.

Well, it's Peachtree East and Peachtree West
And Peachtree Up and Down
But ain't nothing there for you unless
You plan to hang around.
You have to get you a chair in the evening air
Where the Street comes to a fork
And what you'll see on old Peachtree
They ain't got in New York.

Now Peachtree ain't no dead end street;
It runs straight through the town
And the peaches on that famous beat
Ain't free for shaking down.
They got red lips and swivel hips
And they wear their dresses high
And the young men tense and the old men wince
When a Georgia Peach struts by.

It's real high style on the Peachtree Mile
Where the guv'nor takes his lunch.
And the bourbon flows as the evening grows
And the traffic starts to bunch.
Now Sherman burned Atlanta down
And marched on to the sea
But Peachtree Street is still in heat
And that's alright with me.

*1957*

# PART VII

## THIS ROAD SINCE FREEDOM

# THE ATOM

Hark

Vain mortal who has dared to tap
the basic power of the universe,
What have you wrought?

Behold

I stand astride the world.
I am your slave, but you are not my master;
I will not be tamed.

Reflect

I am the spawn of War and Hatred.
The earth founders in its own filth.
I can destroy you all.

*1945*

# THIS ROAD SINCE FREEDOM

America
My native land
How long this road since freedom
How scourged with peril is the path
How bitter is the aftermath
of our sojourn in Edom?
America
My native land
Here on your promises I stand.

O Land
Land of the free
Home of the brave
Will ever there be
for the son of a slave
a place in your scheme:
the American Dream?

O Land
Land I have loved so much
Land I have served so long
When did I fail you
Where did I falter
What is my crime
but my belief
in America?

America
You were my teacher.
In the statement of your law
I heard of justice.
In the dogma of your faith
I learned of mercy.
Enshrined in every public place
I meet your precepts face to face:
Democracy
Equality

Morality
and
Love.

America
You commanded me
and
I surrendered up
the ancient ways,
the ways I knew
before this land
became your land,
before
you gave your law
to be my law,
before
you made your God
to be my God.
The ancient ways,
the laws I kept,
the Gods I knew
are gone.
How can I know
those ways again?
What am I if
I am not American?

Three hundred-fifty years and more
Three thousand miles from the Afric
shore.

A new law
American
A new language
American
A new God
American
American
American
American!

American
But my face is black
What is **black**
What is **white**
What is **man**
What does it mean to be
**American?**

>God made Man
>Out of one clay
>One love
>One will
>One breath
>One plan
>God made Man
>No man above another
>But man to man a brother.

America
In God we trust.
If God is worthy, God is just.
Did God fail in His creative task;
does black some Godly error mask?
If not, then how could God's decree
Be somehow different for me?

>God is the father
>Man is the son
>Men make distinctions
>God makes none.

God made man
What kind of a man
am I?
What kind of a world
is this?
What kind of God
is God?

God is good
The author of mercy
God is just
And righteous altogether.

Where is God?
I wonder if
God saw me
strung high upon a tree
strung high
away up there
embarrassing the summer air
strung high
among the shimmering white magnolias,
the pale white sickening-sweet magnolias?
I wonder if
God saw me suspended there
Somewhere
above God's earth
Somewhere
below God's heaven
Hanging
in the middle of the world,
waiting
for the buzzards overhead
gathered
for a final act of mercy:
to flay my quivering flesh,
to claw my skin away?

**Black skin**
**Black skin**
What does it do
to White men
that robs them of their reason?
Is black some kind of treason
that interrupts
the American Dream
and triggers the hateful

American scream:
Nigger
Nigger
Nigger
**Black Nigger?**

Buzzards
Merciful buzzards
Black like me.

I wonder if
God sent the buzzards out
to pick my bones
and leave them hanging there,
dancing on the air,
bleaching in the sun?

        How white they were
        How white they were
        Your bones among the white magnolias
        Sweet-scented white magnolias
        Above the silent water
        The turgid silent water
        The ever-silent witness
        That tells no tales whatever
        How peaceful were the people
        How gentle and how tranquil
        How silent like the water
        When all your flesh was gone
        When your black flesh was gone
        And all your bones were white.

I wonder if
God saw me burning at the stake
or heard my skin pop open in the flame?
God, did you hear me call the Savior's name
and offer Him my tortured soul to take?

God
did you see my swollen lips
stretched tight and dry
and cracking in the heat
and did you hear the silent prayer
my bloated tongue could not repeat?

There was no sound, I know;
no sound could come.
My prayer, O Lord, was stifled in the flame
each time I tried to say the Savior's name.

No sound could come:
I could not say the words
I heard you say
on Calvary.
No words could come.
The odor of my roasting flesh
filled up my throat.
I retched:
My prayer was vomitus
and agony.

> Forgive them
> For they know not
> What they do.
> What they would do to me
> They do to you.

I wonder if
God saw my shame
when those
who set my pyre
out-raced the flame
to strip my body bare.
The women and the children standing there
looked at my nakedness and cursed my name.
Forgive me!
O forgive me for my shame!
I could not hide myself:

My roasted hands
were pinioned with a chain.

And then they brought a Barlow knife
to rob me of my tree of life
God
Did you see my shame
God
Did you see my tears
when
they hacked my nature off for souvenirs?

      God-a-Mighty
      What a trigger
      On that son-of-a-bitchin' nigger!
      God-damn-looka-there!

Freedom
When will you come at last?
Fearsome has been the past,
bitter the aftertaste,
tragic the human waste.
God grant there yet may be
true freedom for the free.
Justice on every hand
throughout this troubled land.

      True freedom for the free
      Freedom for you and me.

So long this road since freedom,
so dismal has been the way.
Strange flesh in the flames at night,
strange fruit on the trees by day.
Traveling this road alone
so many thousands gone.

      1882, a hundred-thirteen
      So many thousands gone.

O Land
Of white white cotton
With the ax and the plow and the hoe
I felled your forests
I raised your corn
I made your cotton grow.

> 1884, two hundred-eleven
> So many thousands gone.

Your little ones
sucked at a black black breast.
Your young ones
wept on a black black chest.
Black black hands
Laid your old ones to rest,
O Land of Cotton and Corn.

> 1892, two hundred-thirty
> So many thousands gone.

O Land
of golden empire
bound together with ribbons of steel,
I bridged your rivers
I laid your track
I fired your iron wheel.

> 1900, a hundred-fifteen
> So many thousands gone
> 1901, a hundred-thirty
> So many thousands gone!

O Land
when the world's resentments
did threaten your golden store
I bore your colors
I faced the foe
I guarded your sacred shore.

On every star
and every stripe
and on the field of blue
of the flag that waves so gallantly
my blood was shed for you.

> 1919, eighty-three
> So many thousands gone.
> 1933, twenty-eight
> So many thousands gone
> 1964, three to go
> So many thousands gone.

Thank God
this bitter cup
shall pass.
And those who died for freedom
shall at last
be rescued from
the nameless thousands gone
when justice shall have come
into its own.
Yes, write their epitaphs
on parchment scroll
lest America forget
the awesome toll
we paid for liberty
long after we were free.

So long
This road since freedom
This road the martyrs trod
This perilous road from Edom,
we walk this road with God.
So many thousands gone
We do not walk alone.

> We do not walk alone
> God walks beside His own.

America
Of freedom sing
On freedom's road
Let freedom ring
On every hand
Across this land
Let freedom ring
By God's decree
Let freedom ring
For you and me
So long this road since freedom
Let freedom ring!

*1968*

# HARLEM NOCTURNE

## (The Night They Murdered Martin Luther King)

America of thee I sing
Who killed Martin Luther King,
jailed him like a common thief,
whipped his head like a bloody beef,
trailed him with the FBI,
pulled the string and let him die,
mocked the Christian life he led,
put your price upon his head?
Burn Baby! Burn!

Black is black: obscure or great
all Blacks share a common fate:
southern justice in the street,
northern justice on the beat.
Four little girls in Sunday School,
no exceptions to the rule,
Medgar Evers, Malcolm X,
anyone of us is next!
Burn Baby! Burn!

Brothers—one thing left to do:
Burn 'em like they burnin' you.
Rotten flats and rotten meat,
where you live and what you eat.
Honky landlord, Honky store,
get rich off the nigger poor.
Jive you while they cut your throat.
Never let you on the boat!
Burn Baby! Burn!

Rip-off dimes and nickels, too;
send their sons to Harvard U.
Your boys never make the class;
they wind up in Alcatraz.
Every night they take your green,
sack it up and quit the scene,

drive off in their Cadillacs.
Get the bastards off your backs!
Burn Baby! Burn!

Every merchant on the block
got your natural soul in hock.
Mark-up, eighty-five percent:
pay it like you payin' rent.
Get yourself a new Tee Vee;
you have paid for two or three.
Burn the cut-rate liquor store;
cut the rates a little more.
Help yourself to Scotch and gin,
you can't lose what you can't win!
Burn Baby! Burn!

Tomorrow to this hellish slum
watch your so-called leaders come,
ordered by The Man downtown
to get up here and cool it down.
Tellin' you to show your pride,
keep the white folks on your side.
If they dump that crap on you,
burn them white-mouth niggers too!
Burn Baby! Burn!
Burn Baby! Burn!
Burn!

*1968*

# REQUIEM FOR A BLACK NATIONALIST

You are Malcolm X:
Born Malcolm Little
Alias Home Boy
Alias Big Red
Alias Brother Malcolm
Alias Malik Shabazz.

And
You are dead. Quite dead.
Shot down in the Audubon Ballroom,
the day before Washington's Birthday,
the day you were to name the men
you said were set upon your trail
to try to do you in.
Now you are dead.
Shot down in the Audubon Ballroom
late Sunday afternoon.

> Tell it not in Gath
> Publish it not in the streets of Askelon
> Lest the daughters of the Philistines rejoice
> Lest the daughters of the uncircumcised triumph!

You are Malcolm X:
A man destined for tragedy
A man who lived on the edge of violence
A man never reconciled
to your society
or to your condition
or to yourself
A man of tortuous emotions
of violent personal conflicts
A man of impossible yearnings
A black man who wanted
to be a man
in America
And now you are dead.
Dead.

In you, Brother Malcolm
In you, Malik Shabazz
the irresistible force
met the immovable object
and you are dead.

      Brother Malcolm, you were born dead!

There was a bullet made for you:
A bullet with your name
etched in blood,
made the same hour
you quit your mother's womb
Screaming your intent
to be a **man**
in America.

*1965*

# COME BACK,
# MARTIN LUTHER KING

Come Back
Martin Luther King
Pray with me
and
hold my hand
and
help me still the turbulence
the agitation that shakes me
when
I walk the streets of Boston
where once you drew your strength.

O see how quickly there
the people have forgot
the eloquence of outrage
that freedom in the South
was such a paltry thing
And see how strangely there
the people now resent
that freedom in the North
should put them to the test.

Do you hear the mothers
chanting in the streets
**Hail Mary**
**Burn the buses**
**Hail Mary**
**Kill the niggers**
**Hail Mary**
**Let our schools stay white!**

Come Back
Martin Luther King
for
down in your native Georgia
where your name
and where your dream
and

where your followers
made
a Georgia Boy a president
of these United States,
see how boldly there
the Christians in his church
turned the locks
and fired preacher
and split the twice-born congregation
when your Dream
knocked at the church-house door.

Come back
Martin Luther King
Teach us
as once you taught us
to endure;
teach us
as once you taught us
that love
is the price of freedom.

For we are not assured.

The friends we used to know
have long since quit the scene
the responsible people
the proper Bostonians
whose names
gild the log of the Mayflower
are silent and remote
in retirement from the cause
who marched with you
in Selma
keep to their tents
in Boston
and
in a hundred other cities
where

hunger is
and
jobs are not.
There are no voices raised
to give the people hope
or point the way.
There are no shelters raised
for respite from the strife.

Come Back
Martin Luther King
See how
the great cathedrals
that seized your public moment
to gild their own pretensions
are shuttered
from the cause,
are silent now
and voiceless.

Come Back
Martin Luther King
the dreamers you left with your Dream
wake not to the task of the dreaming:
the Dream languishes,
the cock crows,
I hear the tolling of the bells.

**There is no sound of trumpets.**

**When shall we overcome?**

# Epilogue

When Thomas Jefferson read Phillis Wheatley's slender volume of poems, he stated categorically that she was not a poet. Twenty years later he admitted that "of all men I am the last who should undertake to decide as to the merits of poetry." I have similar views regarding my own inability to judge the "merits of poetry." I prefer, however, to remain consistent and, therefore, will not pass judgment on the quality of Eric Lincoln's poetic voice. This does not restrain me from expressing my great admiration for the manner in which Lincoln engages in the intellectual enterprise. While I am content to struggle with several kinds of history, ranging from, say, the general work to the monograph, Lincoln cuts a wide swath across the whole range of humanistic expression: the critical analysis of an institution: *The Black Muslims in America*; the anthology: *A Profile of Martin Luther King, Jr.*; the essay: *Race, Religion and the Continuing American Dilemma*; the novel: *The Avenue, Clayton City* and now, poetry!

One does not need to judge the merits of his poetry (I leave that to the likes of Houston Baker and Helen Vendler) to appreciate the sentiments and the subject matter in this work. The first thing that impresses me is that Lincoln took up this mode of expression well over 40 years ago. Such commitment to any particular genre is commendable. The second thing is the range of concerns that run the gamut from children to the homeless to politics and race. Finally there is feeling and compassion as well as belief and idealism.
I have no doubt that there is much more, and as I continue my struggle to understand poetry this is one of the textbooks from which I hope to learn.

John Hope Franklin
Durham, North Carolina

# C. Eric Lincoln

C. Eric Lincoln was born in Athens, Alabama in 1924. He "grew up" in Trinity High School, a school established by the New England-based American Missionary Association, which he attended from kindergarten through twelfth grade. There was no public high school for black people in Limestone County. Education at Trinity as it was offered by the "Yankee missionaries" was demanding and intensive, and "C. Eric" developed a love and respect for literature and music very early. He wrote his first poem at six, and by the time he graduated from Trinity he had tried his hand at essays, short stories and news reporting as well. At fifteen he was "on his own" in Chicago where many of his most provocative "protest" poems and essays were written.

Lincoln first enrolled at the University of Chicago, but returned south to complete his undergraduate studies at LeMoyne College in Memphis, when he could no longer earn enough at part-time jobs to keep him at the University. He wanted to be a writer, but was advised both at Chicago and LeMoyne to develop a "more practical" interest in a field in which he could more likely earn a living. At LeMoyne he studied sociology and history, returning later to Chicago to study law and religion. He also earned degrees in religion and philosophy at Fisk, and in social ethics and education at Boston University. His first book, *The Black Muslims in America*, published in 1961, has been followed by numerous others. His more recent books include *Race, Religion and the Continuing American Dilemma* (1984), and *The Black Church in the African American Experience* (with Lawrence H. Mamiya) (1990). Lincoln has also published more than 100 essays in professional journals, symposia, and such popular media as *Ebony, Redbook, Pageant, The New York Times Sunday Magazine*, and *Black Collegian*. His first novel, *The Avenue, Clayton City*, won the Lillian Smith Award for best Southern fiction in 1988, and the International Black Writers' Alice Browning Award in 1989. He writes hymns as a hobby and several have been published. *This Road Since Freedom* is his first published collection of poems— a poetic commentary spanning almost 50 years. C. Eric Lincoln is Professor of Religion and Culture at Duke University, and he lives and writes at "Kumasi Hill" in Hillsborough, N.C.